JOHN GIBBS   ABOUT THE AUTHOR

John Gibbs is the writer of several short stories and recently had a memoir published by a regional newspaper.
He is an accountant by profession, now retired and lives with his wife in North Staffordshire.
John has embarked on his first novel which is in the genre of crime fiction.
A combination of a lively wit and vivid imagination is reflected in his literary work.

Those readers that have experienced the military will howl with laughter as they identify their own experience.

ACKNOWLEDGEMENTS

A small number of people helped me on my way as an aspiring writer. In particular, my tutor, David Kinchin at the Writers Bureau. Thanks for your patience and frank criticism. My editor, Kay Leitch for her amazing command of the English language and how it should me written. Last but never least, my wife Stella who suffered many hours of both reading and advising on presentation.

ISBN: 978-1-84944-145-2

British Library Cataloguing in Publication Data.
A catalogue record for this book is available from the British Library.

Published by UKUnpublished

UKUnpublished
.co.uk

www.ukunpublished.co.uk
info@ukunpublished.co.uk

SHORT BACK AND SIDES

The Amusing Experiences of a National Serviceman

by

JOHN GIBBS

SHORT BACK AND SIDES

By John Gibbs

The Amusing Experience of a National Serviceman

Preface:

Conscription in the UK was introduced in 1916. After 1948 it became known as National Service.

Compulsory military service typically required all male citizens to participate for a period of 18 months, which was increased to two years. Usually this was at some point between the age of 18 and late twenties. It was finally disbanded in 1960.

When I was called up in 1954 the prevailing age to vote was twenty-one. Odd I thought. I was old enough to fight for my country and perhaps die, yet not old enough to register my vote!

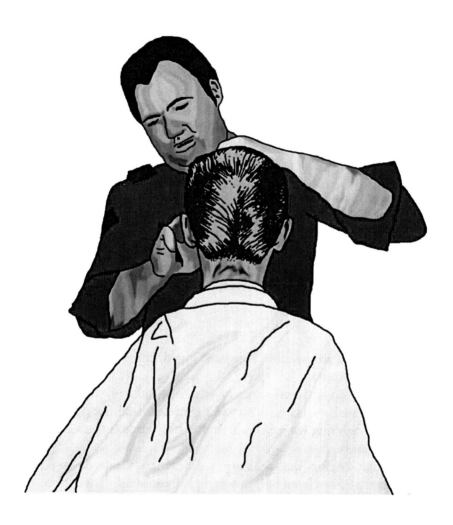

CHAPTER ONE

MY FIRST JOB

I was not destined for a career in rocket science but at least had adequate qualifications that enabled me to go to work wearing a suit. I am utterly useless with my hands and therefore concluded that I must make a living by engaging my brain.

Employment for me commenced on the 20th of August 1951 and I reported to the offices of TM Birkett & Billington Newton Limited, non-ferrous founders and engineers. My job title was apprentice draughtsman The training meant a substantial stint in the drawing office followed by experience in the factory. I could not envisage completing any length of time in the machine shop or foundry and emerging with all my fingers still in place!

***

The chief draftsman was Mr. Sargeant, aged late forties and with the personality of a Rottweiler.

In those far off days the office junior was expected to be at the 'beck and call' of the other staff members. Such tasks included: fetching cigarettes from the corner shop, ordering the lunches from the staff canteen together with any other menial errands.

I was to study for the ordinary national certificate in mechanical engineering and perhaps learn how to accomplish technical drawing.

Draughtsmen would sit on a high stool of wooden construction and face a large drawing board that was equipped with a set square to facilitate the drawing of straight lines. The stool became useful for another equally important role, but more of that later.

I was introduced to the other staff members, who outside the common denominator of engineering, had personalities as diverse as a bag of dolly mixtures.

It was a Monday morning and Alan breezed into the office promptly at nine o'clock. He had recently been demobbed following two years of national service. Alan was of average height, slim and sported the dreaded 'DA' hair-style favoured by the teddy boys. He also spoke in a lingo not familiar with civvies. Expressions like 'chuffed' punctuated every other sentence. Alan had joined the staff as an administrative assistant that he claimed to be well equipped for after the time served in the clerical division of The Royal Army Service Corps.

'How was your weekend?' enquired George.

'Great-- had a few beers with the boys and then went on to see Ken Macintosh at the Victoria Hall. Dead chuffed.'

Next to arrive was Max, real name George Horton. His face had an almost permanent smile, which rounded off his delightful personality. Max was late thirties and an ex regular soldier. He himself had only been back in civilian life for two or three years. Time spent attached to the British Military Mission in Athens had left him with a permanent tan. He routinely opened his newspaper, The 'Daily Telegraph' and spent a few minutes scanning the headlines before getting down to work as an Estimator.

Some time elapsed before the car belonging to Mr Doug Sergeant was seen to arrive in his allotted space just outside the drawing office. The office appeared to light up as he entered, immediately removing his hat to reveal a totally bald dome. There was complete silence, giving the impression of an industrious environment. Little did he know, I thought.

As time passed I more and more became interested in the personal habits and manner of the entirely male work force that I was now part of. I soon observed for example the reading habits of my senior colleagues. Every one other than Alan read a serious newspaper. I quickly copied them and abandoned my copy of The Reveille in favour of the Telegraph. The day I commenced employment, The Times reported the following:

England won the Test match versus South Africa at The Oval.

Geoff Duke was announced as the 1951 junior and senior world champion motorcyclist.

Imperial Tobacco announced a price increase. For a packet of 20 the price rose from 3s 6p to 3s 7p. (The good old days!)

The bank base rate stood at 2%. An incredible statistic, since at the time of writing, its equivalent minimum lending rate is less than 1%.

***

Back to the saga of the drawing office stool I referred to earlier. It was designed for use by a draughtsman and strong enough to support the weight of an adult male.

As Christmas approached and a lighter mood prevailed, Eric, my senior by about seven years, decided that he would provide a little light entertainment at the expense of the junior draughtsman.

One morning while the boss, Mr Sergeant, was absent for the day on business, Eric reminded me of the Birkett tradition of initiating new junior employees. The practice was apparently to lower the individual's trousers and apply Indian Black Ink to the victim's private parts. With a broad grin on his face, while playing to the gallery of onlookers, he remarked that 'Today is the day,' and with that he moved forward in my direction, inkbottle at the ready.

My immediate reaction was to shout, 'please don't do that, you will be hurt.'

Bearing in mind at that tender age I was completely naïve and shy but physically strong, in addition to being much taller and heavier than the comedian now in full flight.

Realising that drastic measures were needed in order to protect my dignity, I reached for the stool and brought it crashing down on the hapless Eric. Fortunately I did not strike his head, otherwise I may well have been writing this book to the accompanying sounds of a harp! Nevertheless, the man was in a sorry state, bleeding from a neck wound and moaning in pain.

'That's the end of my career in engineering,' was my first thought. Office staff that just a moment ago were enjoying the frivolity, were now taking Eric to the medical centre. Thankfully his injuries were found to be superficial but sufficient to cause his exit from work. The stool was now held together with string. The entire audience retreated to their desks with hardly a comment. Needless to say, the ritual of initiation was abandoned for ever.

To my utter amazement when I reported the incident to Mr Sergeant the following day, instead of the sack, I was told to forget the matter. Eric on his return apologised and ironically we became firm friends.

***

I attempted to concentrate on my work and studies as we moved further into the new decade. However, always at the back of my mind was National Service, which loomed ever nearer. My occupation qualified me for deferral. Effectively this meant that I could apply to defer my service until the age of 21. I was not at all anxious to join but preferred to 'get it over with,' However reluctant, I had to prepare myself mentally for military service and what lay ahead. I soon discovered that other exservicemen were anxious to relate their experience.

Max, my elder colleague in the office, advocated joining the Royal Navy and applying for service in the Mediterranean Fleet.

'An absolute doddle,' (military parlance for easy), he commented. 'Fancy sailing up and down the Med as a job?'

'Like being on a permanent luxury cruise,' he continued. Now, for somebody that had never been further than Rhyl that was very appealing. The trouble was that getting accepted into the Navy for national service was very difficult. Entrants were few compared to the other services.

Acting on Max's advice and not to be outdone, I spent my lunch break from work in the recruiting office of The Royal Navy in Cheapside, Hanley, Stoke-on-Trent. It was early May on a beautiful spring day that I walked enthusiastically to discover my fate. No appointment was necessary and a middleaged man dressed in uniform greeted me. He was decked out in garb that could well be that of an Admiral, I thought. His red face suggested he had been at the front of the queue when the 'rum ration' was handed out.

I was pleasantly surprised to learn that they were indeed accepting a number of national service recruits, albeit for special duties. These were explained as 'Morse Code' operators. Evidently there was a distinct lack of 'Morse' communication in the Med.

'No vacancies there,' the officer blurted out as though recognising my ulterior motive. Ah well, so much for the prolonged cruise, I thought. In any event I pursued my interest, I liked the look of the uniform. I was invited to leave my personal details and, if considered suitable, would be contacted for an interview and medical.

I am a Gemini by birth and by nature. Restless, which has meant numerous jobs, cars and sadly, homes. It took three attempts to find the right one. But all of that later!

The frequent changes of mind are evidenced in me forsaking my ambition of becoming a Navel Rating. I was coming up to my 18th birthday when I thought the Army was better equipped for my talents. The dilemma was: which branch of the Army should I apply to?

I had by that time 'seen the light,' and became a born again Christian. Much of this I attributed to the influence of Colin Dale and Arthur Pointon, both fervent members of the Methodist Church, who made up the remaining members of the drawing office.

It was perhaps as a result of my attack on Eric they made me seek forgiveness at the highest level. 'Turn the other cheek,' was the Christian message I had been taught.

During the office tea break I found myself standing next to an ex-national serviceman, Alan.

'Have you made your mind up where to apply to join the mob?' (Military speak for the services) he enquired.

'Not really, I had thought of trying the Navy after speaking to Max.'

Alan, who considered himself as some sort of Guru on National Service, then elaborated on the merits of the lads in khaki.

'Before you start,' I hastened to add, 'I have actually made an application to join the Grenadier Guards.'

'You must be stark raving mad. A friend of mine broke his leg on the assault course.' 'They don't play games at Caterham barracks.'

'Assault course?' I remarked as my bowels started to activate. Apart from the assault on Eric that was the extent of my violent behaviour.

'What's the alternative?' I asked in a feeble voice.

'The Royal Army Service Corps, clerical division,' Alan replied in that, 'know all' manner of his.

'Whatever shall I say to my parents and friends who have been told to anticipate seeing me on leave wearing dress uniform?'

I did not have to ponder my dilemma too long, like a gullible fish I was to be hooked on the bait cast by Alan.

'I have just spent nearly two years at the SHAPE (Supreme Headquarters Allied Powers in Europe) in Fontainebleau, Paris. I was as sick as a parrot to come back,' said Alan.

Now for Alan's secret formula for such a delightful sojourn at the taxpayer's expense.

'You must join the RASC clerks and following basic training in Aldershot, you will be transferred to Willems Barracks for specialist training. Special postings are allotted to those performing well on their course. Such postings could mean service in Oslo, Washington, Paris or Tokyo.'

Alan further cheered me up with his conclusion that I would piss it. Already I could sense the atmosphere as I strolled down the Champs Elyses and gazed at the Eiffel Tower.

Next day was Friday and the weather was typical for October. The rain driven by howling wind lashed into my face as I walked on this occasion to the recruiting office of the Army, situated at the far end of Bethesda Street in Hanley. The same uniformed man that I had met previously invited me to sit down at his desk.

'How can I help, you're the young man hoping to be enlisted in the guards?'

'I've changed my mind,' I blurted out, as my face became a deep red as I observed in a mirror.

'Fancy the Parachute Regiment, I bet?' said the recruiting officer.

'I would like to apply for the 'Royal Army Service Corps,' I said meekly.

'Christ, you know what RASC stands for? Run Away Someone's Coming,' was the response as the corporal stifled a laugh. 'It's your choice if you wish to die of boredom young man,' searching for my file as he talked.

It was now just a matter of waiting, I was informed.

'You will be in before the end of the year,' said the man in uniform, still obviously puzzled by my decision.

The rain had reduced to a light drizzle as I made my way back to work. Despite the weather I was in good spirits as my mind echoed thoughts of my new life in the French capital. Not bad for a lad from the back streets of Burslem, Stoke-on-Trent. I became excited at the prospect of spending a night at La Pigalle instead of Bould Street Methodist church.

***

I was hell bent on topping my course and would devote all my time and energy to attain this. However, it was only a matter of a few days and I was back in civvies mode and vainly trying to forget the wretched Army. I was enjoying my late teens in a familiar environment and had no desire for it to be so crudely interrupted.

Calling up papers were always delivered on a Thursday; once I was into Friday I sighed with relief at the promise of at least one more week of freedom.

It was Thursday the 4th of November 1954 when it finally happened. I arrived home from work at my usual time of six o'clock and was greeted by a wall of silence. The reason being that tucked behind the clock was a buff-coloured envelope with the words, 'On Her Majesty's Service' emblazoned in large print.

CHAPTER TWO

ON MY WAY

It was autumn 1954 and before I embarked on the next phase in my life, I reflected on the important events of that year:

Newcastle went on to win the FA cup.

The Epsom Derby was won by 'Never say Die,' ridden by a young jockey called Lester Piggott.

Jaraslov Drobny won Wimbledon's men's singles final.

Roger Bannister ran the first four minute mile.

Col. Nasser took power in Egypt as prime minister.

Food rationing came to an end, much to the relief of UK citizens.

Other notable sporting events included: the university boat race won by Oxford and the British Open Golf Championship won by the Australian, Peter Thomson.

***

If there was ever such a thing as, *a square peg in a round hole,* this had to be it.

I was brought up in a Methodist family, hence my name, Wesley. Incidentally, I abandoned that name on going into the army. It was sheer embarrassment together with fright that prevented me introducing myself to the teddy boy or Jock, who was built like an oak. My first name John has continued to be used since that time.

I had never been away from home for more than one week and so the prospect of a long period of absence petrified me.

My awareness of National Service and its implications did not occur until I left school and started to work. Looking back, I am amazed that, subject to your abilities or educational achievements, it was just a matter of personal preference as to the particular branch you joined.

***

Over the next few days I was in a state of shock. It didn't help when I walked in the office the day after receiving my call-up papers, to be greeted by Alan, who, with a large grin on his face said. 'The first two years are the worst.'

I contemplated the 'stool job' as an appropriate response but relented on further consideration.

Fortunately the other office members attempted to mitigate my obvious depression.

The Rottweiler, Mr Sargeant, entered, did his Reggie Perrin impression and snapped,' when are you actually leaving?'

I wondered momentarily if I would be able to get my hands on a spare bomb for the bloody man to chew on!

On the Saturday morning prior to leaving for Aldershot, I visited my barber, Mr Tatton, at his shop in Newcastle Street, Burslem. It was a routine visit to attend every other week for my hair cut. As an 18-year old I was very proud of my thick dark hair held in place with Brylcreem.

As my turn came round, I raised from my seat alongside the remaining clients and took my place in the barber's chair. Mr Tatton placed a cape round my shoulders and enquired,

'The usual young man?'

'No, I am going into the Army next week, Mr Tatton, I better have it a bit shorter.'

'Oh dear,' he responded as though I had given news of a terminal illness. After approximately ten minutes I was invited to look in the mirror to view his handiwork. Gosh, my girlfriend will not approve of that, I thought. I considered wearing a large hat to hide the damage but settled for a bunch of flowers in order to distract the girl's attention.

***

On the 18th of November 1954, following a tearful farewell, I collected my suitcase and set off to catch the bus. My destination was Stoke-on-Trent railway station where I was to join the train bound for London. My much loved uncle Jack was to accompany me to the railway station.

The weather that November morning matched my mood. It was still dark at seven and the rain bounced off my face, disguising the tears. I felt hopelessly lonely as I hugged my aged pal, picked up my case and leapt on the departing train. I did not look back. I slung my luggage on to the rack above and slumped into a vacant seat.

Sod it, I thought: at least the weather should be better in Paris.

I had made the train journey only once previously on a school trip and reckoned it would be at least three hours before I spotted the twin towers of Wembley Stadium and then only a short trip into Euston station. In between thoughts of home and friends, I contemplated my life as a soldier.

On arrival at Euston I was to use the tube train to transfer to Waterloo station. I was immediately reminded me of a scene from the film, 'Brief Encounter' starring Leslie Howard. Another depressing experience I thought, quickly turning my mind back to current matters.

The travel instructions, which had been enclosed with the calling-up documents, indicated that from Waterloo station I was to embark on the final part of the trip, destination: Aldershot, Hants, home of the British Army. I would be met at the station and taken to the selection barracks in Farnham. What they failed to mention was that together with other unfortunate lads we would be herded like cattle onto a truck, which would shake the shit out of you!

As I gazed out of the window the scenery changed from the grey mist of the industrial towns to various shades of green and brown as the engine sped south through the countryside.

I pondered again what my first day would have in store. How was I to cope with the inevitable bad language and witnessing the effects of heavy drinking? And incidentally, I did not like being told what to do!

With the screeching of brakes and clouds of steam arising from the Royal Scotsman I arrived at Euston station. I was now becoming extremely nervous. A condition that Alan later defined as 'shitting bricks.' Walking along the station platform and struggling with a heavy case, I noticed a smartly dressed soldier wearing a red peak cape bearing the words, Military Police. The Military Police had a fierce reputation and were always on the lookout for any wayward behaviour involving service personnel. I was sure that the stare he gave me was capable of removing my civilian veneer and revealing a new recruit. I shuddered as I walked past.

John Gibbs

It was now only a matter of hours before I ceased being Mr John Gibbs, apprentice draughtsman and Methodist local preacher, and became S/23092158 Private Gibbs, Royal Army Service Corps.

CHAPTER THREE

THE ROYAL ARMY SERVICE CORPS

One of the responsibilities of the RASC is the provision of clerical service to the Staff. Initial training was carried out at Blenheim barracks near Aldershot. Soldiers were primarily required to develop their military skills in weapon training and field-craft and then be proficient in their trade.

It was 1918 before the corps received the Royal prefix for its service in the First World War. It is divided into Transport and Supply branches.

The RASC subsequently merged with the Transportation and Movement Control Service of the Royal Engineers and became known as the Royal Corps of Transport.

***

The train journey between Waterloo and Aldershot was uneventful. The view from the carriage window went unheeded as nerves took over. Clearly a number of passengers of my age and carrying suitcases were destined for a similar fate. On arrival I peered round the surrounding car-park. Within seconds a voice, obviously not opera trained, shouted,' RASC over here.' A uniformed man with a single stripe on his shirtsleeve was observed pointing to an armoured truck. I found myself sitting alongside other young men, all-staring at the scene beyond and with the appearance of cattle en route to the abattoir. It seemed like only minutes before we paused at the Guardroom of Blenheim barracks A soldier on sentry duty, after speaking briefly with the driver, raised a steel barrier and allowed us to proceed. The vehicle eventually came to a halt and everyone was ordered to step down.

'Get fell in over there,' was the instruction. The accompanying lance corporal was obviously not a graduate in English language I mused. Next stop was to the front of a single story building that could well have been constructed to accommodate soldiers who fought in the 'Crimean war.' We, together with approximately 50 other new recruits, had been marched there in a scene reminiscent of prisoners on their way to the Gas Chambers.

***

Day one as a National Serviceman was to include, registration and issue of a Regimental Pay Book, issue of uniform, allocation of sleeping quarters and a hair cut. Oh and perhaps very late in the day, food may be offered.

I glanced at my Pay Book. It was emblazoned with my regimental number, S/23092158. It is said that very few servicemen forget their number. How can you? When some silly sod of a sergeant threatens to cut your balls off if you do: for most purposes only the last three digits are used.

Other statistics read: height, 6ft 1in; weight, 11st 4lbs: religion, Methodist and next of kin, mother. My father had died in 1953.

Issue of Army uniform from the Quartermasters stores was the first task and first experience of the crass stupidity of the military. Written language used by the army is frankly absurd. The habit of using expressions back to front is an example.

The 'Kit' as they describe it was selected from a 'check-list' and thrown across a wooden counter roughly in the direction of the 'squaddie.' It comprised, battle dress, overcoat (greatcoat), shirts, socks and underwear designated, 'drawers cellular,' I ask you? In addition I was given webbing belt, sorry, belt webbing, gaiters and the all important 'mess-tins.' These were a substitute for a plate, as Royal Doulton had failed to deliver chinaware to Aldershot.

As trolleys were not provided, soldiers were then ordered to form an orderly queue outside, where we would be provided with an accommodation block number. With kit piled high we were then marched to our sleeping quarters. 'Not exactly The Ritz, I thought on arrival.

I was now thoroughly pissed off and starving. We were allotted a bed in a room that, apart from the floor that was shining like an early morning sunrise, was a hellhole. A stove pot in the middle of the room provided the only heating.

Still wearing civilian clothes we were then taken for a regimental hair cut. As we marched towards the building block that contained the barber's shop, I noticed a number of my fellow servicemen had the popular 'Ducks Arse' hair style and were wearing long jackets and 'brothel creeper' shoes. The term brothel creeper stemmed from the design of a leather 'upper' with a very thick rubber sole. Now for a laugh, I thought, as we were ordered to halt outside the single- story building. They ought to have been sensible like me and had their hair cut short.

A long line of forlorn looking young men was being directed to a less than salubrious barber's shop. I was soon sitting on a wooden seat and facing a blank wall that appeared to have been last decorated around the time of William the Conqueror. No cape was placed around my shoulders. No class, I thought and blurted out feebly, **short back and sides please.'** The uniformed soldier holding an electric shaver and hovering to my rear let out a mouthful of abuse that would not be acceptable on a building site!

'Are you effing kidding?' was the remark. He then proceeded to grab a few strands of hair with the other hand and applied the cutting tool. The process was akin to a sheep being sheared. I glanced at my reflection in the window as I rejoined my comrades. The veins stood out on the side of my head and the remnants of hair comprised a small tuft that hung over my brow.

A tall gangling figure of a youth said,

'What did you make of that, then?' Only his cockney accent enabled recognition as a member of the same billet. The DA and Drapes seemed light years away.

The one small consolation was the announcement that we were to be fed prior to 'turning in' for the night. We were instructed to 'get fell in' yet again before being marched to the Cookhouse (see restaurant). My mouth started to water as I envisaged starting the evening meal with the soup de jour followed by a steak medium rare with mixed salad. A glass of house red would also be very acceptable, I thought. However, reality was not up to expectations. Mess Tins in hand I was paraded to the Cookhouse where I sampled buffet service, military style. There was no soup left, I was informed as I held out my eating utensils, rather like Oliver Twist.

Something remotely resembling a burger was tossed in the can followed by watery looking veg. Frankly my boxer dog would have expressed little interest in the dish.

No wine either, only water and my crude behaviour meant I couldn't call on Jesus for a quick miracle.

Following the eating episode we were allowed to make our own way back to the appropriate barrack room. As I walked alongside an equally doleful soul, he enquired, 'How did you find your steak?'

'Hiding behind a chip,' I chortled. A sense of humour again came to the rescue.

CHAPTER FOUR

BASIC TRAINING

I was told the following day, that selection and basic training was to be for duration of two weeks. Those chosen to work as clerks would then be transferred to Willems barracks, Aldershot, for enhanced regimental and trade training.

The first morning of army life was an experience I will never forget. At 5.30am, sorry, 0530, hours. I awakened to what I assumed was the outbreak of war. At precisely that time, the barrack room door was flung open and in marched the duty sergeant, a huge stick in his hand. He proceeded to thrash the bottom of the nearest bed causing a loud bang and an attack of diarrhoea among the hapless young men. This action was accompanied by the yell,
  'Get your feet on the deck.'
  In fear and trembling I joined the stampede to the Washroom. There were sinks with wall mirrors placed at intervals along the side of the room-ablutions. Men fought for a glimpse of their face which may become visible as body in front rocked from side to side in order to gain on the rest. It was sheer farce as naked men in the freezing cold attempted to wash and shave.

***

During those first two weeks the Army's task was to familiarise the rookies with an understanding of army rules and regulations in addition with regimental procedures. In that short time I was to experience a conversion more dramatic than St Paul.

When and how to salute, was an early lesson. The corporal responsible for that days training performed a demonstration.
  'Longest way up, shortest way down' was the order as a salute was carried out. Remember, only officers of commissioned rank must be saluted on sight and only if you are wearing headgear. Got that, laddie?' was added for good measure. All quite mad, I thought. Marching/Drilling discipline, which is commonly referred to as 'square bashing' is performed on the parade ground.

This is an area of tarmac resembling a car park and approximately the size of a football pitch.

I had to learn on command to stand to attention, stand easy, how to march in time and with the correct coordination of arms and legs. It was very embarrassing to find my left leg for example shot off in the same direction as my left arm.

'You're marching like a load of ruptured ducks,' was one memorable comment.

The really hard part though, was drilling while carrying a rifle. The secret was for all movements to be made to a system of timing that the student soldier repeated to himself. In my case it proved not to be foolproof.

Fixing a bayonet to your rifle was an art in itself. The bayonet was to be attached to the end of the barrel by placing it in position and securing it with a sharp manoeuvre of the hand. All to a count of three, of course.

My first brush with army discipline occurred as a result of the wretched bayonet fixing procedure.

It happened during what had become a routine 'square-bashing' lesson. I was positioned on the front rank as the drill sergeant shouted the command 'order arms.' The instruction to 'fix bayonets' followed. At this point it was intended that the rifle should be lifted using one hand and then the weapon transferred to sit on the left shoulder.

'One, One, two, three, I murmured as I removed the bayonet from my belt and attempted to attach this to the rifle.

I had not secured the bloody thing when the next order was given, which in consequence saw the missile fly up in the air and in the direction of the poor sods standing on the back row (rank). I dared not look myself but was later told that I had nearly decapitated private Jones.

I froze as the drill sergeant bellowed instructions to the corporal assisting the parade, 'arrest that effing stupid, orrible little man.' I was confronted by the corporal, brought to attention and promptly stormed off to the Guardroom.

Visiting the Guardroom was not a pleasant experience. The sheer humiliation was enough to consider desertion but AWOL (Absent Without Leave) was rather frowned on in the military and I feared the firing squad.

I was formally charged to appear before the CO (Commanding Officer) at 0900 hrs the next day; meanwhile, I was allowed to return to my squad.

'Attention, quick march at the double,' ordered the orderly sergeant. I had been standing outside the CO's door with just one week of service to my credit. I came to a halt in front of the Captain's desk and saluted as I was ordered to attention.

'Remove cap,' barked the sergeant.

I was referred to the 'Queens Regulations' that is the army bible and contains the orders and procedures relating to military discipline.

The sergeant then read out the charge.

'Private Gibbs, you are charged that, subject to good order and military discipline, that you on the morning of the 25th November 1954 did unlawfully and recklessly cause a bayonet to exit your rifle in a manner which could have caused serious injury to other soldiers.'

'What do you have to say in your defence?' uttered the acting officer in a somewhat plummy accent.

'Sorry sir,' was my attempt at remorse.

'Seven days CTB (Confined to Barracks), in addition you must report to the Guardroom at 1800 hours for additional duties. March him out, sergeant.' As there was not a stool handy I was dismissed

***

The extra duties that were part of my punishment are known as 'Jankers' in army speak. The task I was given had no end value or usefulness. Together with other poor sods I reported to the Guardroom at 1800 hrs The corporal in charge gave the customary order to 'get fell in.' In sheer terror we then awaited specific instructions detailing the work.

My opinion at this stage was that all non commissioned officers attended night school for a course in stupidity and bullying. I was ordered to clean a table GS (General Service).

'I want it clean enough to eat off' shouted the diminutive figure with two stripes on his arm.

Little man syndrome, I concluded. Tools of the trade were a bucket of hot water and a large scrubbing brush. The table was constructed of wood fitted on top of an iron frame. Not the sort of thing you would find in Christie's saleroom.

My father once said, 'Son, if you are told to dig holes, make sure you dig good ones.' With that advice in mind I grabbed the brush and set about transforming the appearance of a table GS. After about two hours, like a spaniel dog, I presented the finished article to the corporal. This particular piece of dining room furniture was still not up to Royal standards, but in my opinion spotlessly clean!

'Bloody filthy,' he shoved a finger in my face and screeched, 'clean it.' The finger was apparently to indicate a speck of dirt taken from the underside. With that, the gentleman filled a gigantic shovel with coke and proceeded to shower the contents all over my handy-work.

I was utterly gob-smacked. I could cheerfully have shot the silly bugger, but the thought of being incarcerated in Colchester military prison served to deter me. Was this an attempt at severe humiliation or the army's idea of discipline? At the end of the seven days I vowed to become adroit at bayonet fixing.

My first weekend spent in the army reduced me to a mental wreck. Weekends at home were usually devoted to a strict routine comprising: a haircut, which alternated with a trip to the local baths for my one bathe of the week. This was sheer luxury compared to the tin bath that I squeezed into that I had strategically placed in front of dying embers in the early hours of the morning.

Sport featured prominently on the itinerary, as I supported both local teams, Stoke City and Port Vale. As their matches were always arranged alternatively it made it possible to watch both.

At that time I was very involved in church activities and therefore the remainder of the weekend would be cleansing the soul in readiness to take on the military.

All this was in stark contrast to the life of a newly recruited national service man.

***

Initially you were not allowed to leave the camp during the weekend. Weekend passes were later granted for either a 36- or 48-hour leave. A 'roster' of weekend duties was displayed in a prominent location in various parts of the barracks. Groups of anxious young men would gather late on Friday afternoons to learn their fate.

One of the advantages of being tall is the ability to see over those in front. Necks were craned in search of the duties that had been allocated. There it was, Pvt Gibbs Attend Commanding Officers, garden. Report to your duty sergeant at 1400 hrs on Saturday the 20th and 1430 hrs on Sunday the 21st November. I bet he's got a big sodding garden I thought with some venom. Why can't the bugger live in a two up and two down like the rest of us?

John Gibbs

The Commanding Officer enjoyed the privilege of a five- bedroom detached house situated across the road from the camp's main- gate. The garden area was approximately a quarter of an acre with a rolling lawn surrounded by a neatly trimmed hedgerow. Large Oak trees stood majestically at intervals round the perimeter. And what do Oak trees do in the autumn? Shed bloody leaves profusely and continuously.

There were four of us assigned to garden duty and the sergeant in charge, in a voice designed to frighten the shit out of 'Genghis Khan,' shouted out his requirements in detail.

'Atten-Shun,' he called.' Right you orrible little men.' I could now smell his Woodbine-laden breath as he continued. 'One: collect fallen leaves and remove to compost heap. For your guidance a compost heap is a pile of garden rubbish. Two: water the flowerbeds located round the edge of main lawn. Then mow lawns to a grass height not exceeding two inches.' In 1954 they were not afforded the benefit of sophisticated equipment.

'Any questions?' asked the sergeant. It was starting to drizzle with rain as he put the question. Private L'Borde, an insignificant little man, still standing to attention, spoke.

'It's raining sergeant,' as if revealing the outbreak of a third world war,' what do we do about watering the plants?'

The sergeant, whose blood pressure must now read 200/150, bawled, 'wear your effing great coat.'

I could not believe what I had just heard. I fought in vain to keep a straight face. This was a stage hall joke but delivered in all seriousness. At least it provided a little light relief to my otherwise miserable weekend.

I was IC (In Charge) of leaf collection. It was frankly like peeing into the wind. As I dumped the bucket of leaves, I returned to my patch to discover that more bloody leaves had fallen. If ever I have to do national service again, I swear I will ensure that I do not join in the autumn.

As I toiled alongside my equally disenchanted comrades, I recalled a popular song of the day. I hummed the tune of the Nat King Cole hit, 'A blossom fell from off a tree.'

The rain had stopped and the light was fading fast. I thought for one horrible moment they would issue gardening personnel with torches.

The duty sergeant barked out an order to 're-group.' The weary gardeners carried out the order enthusiastically. It was back to the barrack room for a quick wash and heading off to 'The Ritz' as it had become known.

I peered down at the contents of my Mess Can, where a burnt sausage was swimming towards me in a sea of gravy. However, after what I had endured in the time before this was bliss.

The following Friday was the 'Passing Out Parade.' On the Thursday night prior I collapsed on to my bed having emerged from the 'bull session.' That involved the pressing and ironing of my uniform together with the 'bullying' of boots. I could now handle an iron with some dexterity. Mother would have been proud of me, I thought.

On the morning of the 'Passing Out Parade,' young men, polished and gleaming, assembled on the square.

Judging from the yawns and rubbing of eyes, little sleep had been had. They compared their blackened fingers as they cursed the habit of' bullying' kit.

Second Lieutenant, Burrel facing his men.

'Now then chappies, lets see a jolly good show from you today.'

Private Dixon, in a thick Glaswegian accent, said, 'silly prick' which reflected a consensus of opinion.

The Lieutenant was a national service officer that had graduated from Oxford obtaining a commission at 'Mons,' the equivalent of Sandhurst

His wan complexion suggested he had spent too much time reading books.

The parade concluded with the salute taken by the officer commanding the battalion.

Instructions were read out indicating that I as part of the clerical division I would be transferred to Willems Barracks for more intensive training.

***

CHAPTER FIVE

WILLEMS BARRACKS

The barracks where I was to spend the next six weeks was constructed between 1856-59 and known originally as the 'West Cavalry Barracks' and renamed Willems in 1909 after the cavalry victory in 1794 during the French Revolutionary Wars

The barracks comprised: Guardroom and cells plus four two-storey troop stalls, officers' mess and a riding school.

Feeling rather like doomed sheep we arrived at the gateway to Willems Barracks, which faces the Farnborough Road and still survives today.

***

Ponder for a moment where you would least like to spend a holiday or indeed any time at all.

This 'hell hole,' designed to accommodate horses in the eighteenth century was to be my home for a while. My view was that little had changed. For example, instead of hay, they served shredded wheat as a staple diet and gaslights had been replaced by electricity, but little else.

An army truck carrying approximately a dozen squaddies halted outside the tall grey buildings that were described as barracks. A large three-storey building stood on both sides of a narrow road. The surface of the road was clearly well worn and I doubted that the local authority had adopted it.

Iron steps with railings gave access to the floors above. It was these that had been adapted to provide living quarters for the new recruits.

Our feet hit the uneven surface as we jumped down from the lorry struggling not to part company with a 'kit bag.' As luck would have it, I was allocated a billet on the top floor of this monstrosity. I had by now become friends with a lad from Southampton, named Rod Bryant. We had discovered a mutual interest in football and had similar taste in music. It eased the gloom a little to hear the 'striped uniform' called Rod to the same accommodation.

With considerable effort I placed the khaki-coloured canvas bag over my shoulder and ascended to room eighteen. I avoided looking down through the open staircase. I suffer from vertigo, which is not conducive to heights.

I have always harboured a deep unease arising from a change in domestic routine. My early background as a church-going well-behaved young man was in sharp contrast to many of my group. As I could not escape the swearing and the bawdy actions I was often left in a state of despair. This feeling of insecurity was responsible for me 'sticking like shit to a blanket' when I did make friends.

On the first full day at Willems barracks, I joined one of three squads that were to undergo intensive training.

The daily routine for those initial three weeks comprised: drill (square bashing), physical training, and weapon training and rifle practice on the 'firing range.'

I hated physical training and recalled my school days. A gruff voiced instructor would appear. As he spoke, the muscles on his body bounced like a cork on a rough sea. I was not alone in wishing his premature demise.

Training would be by means of lectures, films and demonstrations. It culminated with the trade training, held in the classrooms.

Monday to Fridays were long hours of activity that continued after the end of the so-called working day at 1700 hours.

Following a break to take on what was roughly described as food, a series of extra or general duties were the norm. As that first day's orders were read out I narrowly missed out on the Cookhouse. I had looked forward to washing up dishes and greasy pans for three hours!

'Private Gibbs, spud bashing, get over there,' yelled the NCO in charge. Six of us were directed to a building that would once have doubled up as a cow shed. In one corner of this huge room that was last painted by Picasso, was a mountain of potatoes. Tools of the trade were a knife and a bucket the size of a petrol drum. The task was described as simple: peel 'tators' and place in bucket ready for collection.

It was a dauntless task, as every bucket load peeled gave way to another load that took its place.

Feeling very tired and still hungry I contemplated scoffing a nice plate of sandwiches while sitting in front of the television. No such luck! Instead, at about nine pm we were allowed to return to billet. Refreshment was a chocolate biscuit bought earlier in the day from the NAFFI and washed down with a mug of water.

There was still work to be done as kit had to be laid out for inspection the following morning. Boots required the traditional bullying. This process I should explain involves wrapping a duster around your finger on one hand and with the remainder of the duster clasped into a ball and in the palm of your hand, you're ready to go. An argument would rage as to which polish was best, Cherry Blossom or Kiwi?

It was not a particularly healthy pursuit as it meant spitting on to the toecap and then rubbing in small circles on to the boot, which would produce a gleaming finish.
The price paid was a badly stained index finger.

The Kit layout of a soldier must adhere to a high standard and conform to a predetermined pattern. For example, the blankets had to be folded and boxed. Some men chose to sleep on the floor in order not to disturb the bedclothes overnight. The duty sergeant's inspection the following morning would very often cause, a bout of nerves.

***

The tallest members of a parade would always occupy the front rank. Although not the tallest, I was inevitably at the front and staring into the miserable face of the drill sergeant He would be standing to attention with a drill stick held under the armpit.
When the moment arrived for my personal inspection I was close enough to detect the tobacco fumes on his breath. His eyes like an eagle about to devour its prey would shift up and down my person I experienced the onslaught of diarrhoea as he stooped down to wipe his stubby finger on my boot.
The sergeant proceeded to shove it up my nose while exclaiming, 'dirt.'
I thought, God no, its back to scrubbing tables GS for me!
Fortunately, I was merely issued with a warning. My boots reflected his horrible face as he proceeded down the line: such was the extent of the dirt.

***

After two weeks at Willems I was granted my first weekend pass. They were issued for duration of either thirty-six or forty-eight hours I yearned to visit home but this was impossible in less than forty-eight hours.

However, I was determined to capitalise on my freedom and decided on a jaunt to London. The journey to Waterloo station would take under two hours and by catching the early morning train. I was in the metropolis by noon. My army mates, to my surprise opted to stay in Aldershot.

It was a Saturday and, as I scanned the morning newspaper, I noticed that Stoke were visiting Portsmouth. That can't be too far away, I thought and quickly changed trains for my football feast. So far so good, I thought. Despite being on my own, I enjoyed the trip, avoiding assassination when standing in a sea of blue scarves I cried out in vain for the team in red and white stripes.

The famous centre forward, Dougie Read, was playing that day and was a joy to behold.

I arrived back in London before seven pm and as I was no rush to return to military life I ventured into a cinema after tucking in to the largest plate of fish and chips I could find. I watched the Glen Miller story for the second time. I was hooked on the Miller sound.

Depression set in as I approached Aldershot train station. When I arrived back at the barracks I reported to the Guardroom, as required, before clambering up the stairs to my billet. My face lit up when scattered on top of my bed was a pile of coins and a note, 'lucky bastard.' I had forgotten that I had entered, contrary to my Methodist doctrine, the football sweep. My winnings were sufficient to pay for a few cheese rolls at the NAFFI canteen. Not exactly The Ritz but most welcome.

The ensuing week was uneventful apart from an unexpected meeting. Standing in a queue while waiting for breakfast to be served, I recognised the face of John Fishwick. We had attended the same school, albeit that he was a year ahead of me. It transpired that John was on the permanent staff of the training section and worked in the postings office.

With my eyes on a dream trip to Paris I was anxious to discover where the special postings had been recently.

'Am I in for gay Paris?' I laughed.

'You're bloody ambitious as ever,' joked John. I was nevertheless cheered up when I was informed that over the last few months there had been a select few that had been sent to Washington, Tokyo, Oslo and Paris. By this time John was in position to be served and I departed with the words, 'Catch up with you later.'

***

It was clear that an isolated opinion was not going to change the training methods of the British Army and therefore I had to adapt.

I was bored rigid during the first three weeks of square bashing, weapon training and physical training.

Weeks seemed like an eternity and I longed for the weekends to provide less restriction and a change of environment. My first free weekend following my London trip, saw me in the company of several of my pals and a venture into the town of Aldershot.

The majority view was to visit the cinema followed by the gastronomic delights of the NAAFI .

The NAAFI building is a large rambling property that exists in the main for the recreational activities of soldiers.   In addition to catering facilities, it provides a   squash court, a gym and a bar/lounge area.

Showing at the town's main picture house was the famous film, *On the Water Front* starring Marlon Brando.   The young Brando gave an award-winning performance to the delight of the largely military audience.

Come six o'clock we were all starving and moved like a herd of elephants in the direction of the NAAFI. Unfortunately, half of the force's personnel of this garrison town thought likewise.

I collected a tray and joined the long queue to be served. I was a few feet away from presenting my tray to a chef who was currently involved in demonstrating his skill in flipping numerous sausages on to a plate while simultaneously frying an egg. Suddenly I became aware of a soldier in uniform who had jumped the queue ahead of me. Not the done thing, I thought. I turned to Rod, who was standing behind me and enquired,' did you see that rude bugger jump in? After waiting for an hour, that's pissed me off,' I was about to address the offender.

'I wouldn't say anything, 'declared a sheepish looking Rod.

'Why ever not?' I whispered.

'See that dark red berry folded under his epaulette.'

I glanced at the familiar hat and distinguishing cap badge.

' He's a paratrooper and will murder us lot in the pursuit of a few extra chips.'

'Oh,' I said and immediately regained my composure.

We trudged wearily back to barracks and made the compulsory visit to the Guardroom to be checked in. It was shortly before midnight and the time the pub revellers meandered back, singing as they swayed from side to side and shouting the occasional obscenities to anyone within earshot.

***

The commencement of week four at Willems was the start of the clerical training. It was this aspect of my duties that would be tested and the results determine my subsequent posting. It's either Grimsby or Paris for you lad, I thought.

The lectures were held in a large one-storey building that was divided into classrooms. The rooms would accommodate approximately thirty men were light and airy and beyond the expected standard.

I learned to 'touch type' at forty-five words per minute, a skill I still find useful.

Instruction in army administration was another principle subject provided.

The three weeks of clerical training passed quickly and I was soon contemplating the results. I was fairly confident of good marks in reward for my honest endeavours. I had even managed to control my nerves during the typing test.

During that time I had obtained a forty-eight-hour weekend pass. I managed a trip home to the north midlands, which was like manna from heaven. I spent two days being utterly spoiled on stodgy delightful food and affection.

I was greeted at Stoke station by my long-suffering girl friend that led me to a waiting taxi en route to her parents' home.

Young men are totally selfish and never for one moment considered that my own family may wish to see me. The time flew and the return journey by coach quickly became a reality. At least I was able to defer my leaving until eleven o'clock on the Sunday evening. The overnight trip in the company of a coach load of bawdy soldiers was not a prospect I relished. I was due back in camp at 0600hrs and therefore I endeavoured to sleep as a means of escape.

CHAPTER SIX

THE POSTINGS

It was early March 1955 and about a hundred anxious looking Service Corps personnel were assembled to learn their fate.

I was on the back row of a large lecture hall and displaying all the signs of nervous anxiety that even images of the Champs Elysee failed to quell. Captain Drew, the officer in charge of the proceedings, sat with his two NCOs and looking quite nonchalant. The trio were seated on a platform that looked down on the gathering of students.

Captain Drew rose from his seat and peered over the top of his spectacles at the manuscript laid out on the lectern to his side. My destiny lay within.

With a pulse rate of what must have been over one hundred and perspiration on my brow, I froze. The officer looked directly at me, and then appeared to hesitate a fraction before making the announcement.

S/23092158 Private Gibbs-Oo La La ,I sang to myself.

Cough, pause: 91%, Special Posting, Head Quarters Ack-Ack Command, Dover.

We filed out of the room and all attempts to console me with silly humour failed. I was crestfallen and could not wait to consult my friend in the postings office, John Fishwick.

***

John looked up from his desk as I strutted into his office. With a sheepish look on his face he greeted me with,' Hi John, what can I do for you?'

I considered a suggestion of suicide and then realised of course that John could not influence my posting.

'Dover,' I blurted out.

'Its just bad luck,' John pleaded and added that for some reason Dover is indeed the special posting.

' Perhaps they thought you had an interest in castles,' he quipped.

I thought that he was now pushing his luck too far in not understanding the main attraction of Paris as opposed to the Kent coast.

'I don't want to go,' I added, 'do I have an option?'

'You can join the draft to BAOR (British Army of the Rhine).'

'Right,' I replied, 'done.'

***

The day following the encounter with Captain Drew, the course members were scattered far and wide without grace or favour.

There were sad farewells as we all in turn engaged in vigorous handshakes and back slapping. I read the notes provided and I was pleased to see that my friend Rod Bryant was also destined for Germany. My initial posting within the BOAR, was to the Royal Army Service Corps Training Wing at Sennelager, West Germany.

Following embarkation leave I was to report to the transit camp in Boredon, Hants. From there we would be taken via London Victoria to the port of Harwich in Essex.

A troopship would then make the overnight crossing to the Hook of Holland. 'The bloody North Sea in winter I fumed.' A, tad rougher than Hanley Park Lake I bet!'

We packed kitbags the size of a young bull and scrambled on board in search of a bunkbed. It was early March when I entered a new phase of my life in the military. I got off to a particularly bad start! The bunkbeds were constructed hammock style. That is, one bed on top of another, causing the bed to swing when someone climbed on.

My stomach and rough seas do not go well together. We set sail and in the early hours of the morning I was struggling to sleep. The waves were horrendous, causing the ship to toss about like a rodeo rider. I became violently sick and quite naturally turned my head over the bedside as my guts erupted, spraying its contents on the hapless fellow in the bottom bed. I thought that after four months in the army that I had heard every swear word invented. Evidently not as the Scottish gentleman, who was the victim of my seasickness uttered the vilest verbal onslaught accompanied by threats to my life. Within minutes his face was inches away from mine but then I think the smell caused him to back off.

While questioning my parentage he sulked off in the direction of the loo in order to freshen up.

As we disembarked the following morning, my legs felt like jelly and I was still very nauseous. There was a sergeant shouting instructions that made my head pound further. I looked round to see if I recognised anyone from my draft and fortunately two former members of my course were slightly ahead. Despite all attempts to create some semblance of order it was extremely difficult with several hundred men involved.

'We are to assemble over there under the red banner,' said one of the lads.

The scene was like a huge cattle market with bodies jostling for position in response to loud voices. Certainly the journey to Dover would have been easier than this, I conceded. After standing amid a large gathering of weary-looking men I heard the magic words of,

'You lot over there for the red train.'

'God,' organisation at last I thought.

I joined the train that would take me from the Hook of Holland via Monchengladbach to the town of Paderborn in West Germany.

I found a vacant seat, dumped my kitbag and collapsed into my seat. My mind immediately wandered back to my embarkation leave; I had lapsed back into civilian life within a few days of arriving home. The prospect of rejoining my unit for a long stay in a foreign city, I found daunting. It was to be at least six months before I would be allowed home leave.

The fact that my much talked about holiday in the French capital had aborted did not help the mood.

My mother expressed the view, that being in Paris may place me in moral if not mortal danger. I assume she arrived at that opinion following her weekly visit to the 'Christian Fellowship' meeting.

Bearing in mind that it was still only ten years since the Second World War ended, Germany was still regarded as potentially unsafe. After much sorrow and regret I dressed in uniform and checked my travel documents, which would take me to the transit camp based in Boredon in Hants. It was a very reluctant national serviceman that bade farewell to friends and family to embark on the next stage of my army life.

The train that was used to ferry army personnel to Boredon was infamously given the name, 'the Boredon Bullet.' The sarcasm was derived from the pace at which this antiquated transport travelled between London Waterloo and a railway station in Hampshire that Wyatt Earp might feel at home in

As is customary, The Bullet sidled into Boredon where numerous weary men alighted. Boredon cannot be described as bustling and therefore the trucks parked outside the station were easily visible. Three vehicles in convoy then made the short journey to the barracks.

Although not exactly Butlins standard, the accommodation was reasonable. Discipline was also more relaxed for the short stay prior to embarkation. The time was devoted to administration and further medical checks.

The fateful day arrived for the trip to Sennelager via Victoria station and the port of Harwich in Essex. With true military precision troops were moved en-masse to be dispersed throughout the British Zone of Western Germany.

***

The train journey between the Hook of Holland and Paderborn seemed to take for ever. I peered out of the windows and I realised I was now on foreign soil. We passed through Eindoven in Holland where the giant electronics business of Phillips can still be seen today. Travelling through the German countryside I noticed hundreds of what appeared to be small craters that had been grassed over. I was later to learn that they were the result of wartime bombing that had left its mark on the landscape.

Again, like clockwork, The Royal Corps of Transport performed admirably and were waiting at the railway station to take us on the final leg of the journey to the Royal Army Service Corps Training Wing and 138 Supply Company.

***

Sennelager is a village in Germany that forms part of the city of Paderborn. It is notable by the presence of a British Army barracks, where I was to stay. It is so vast and with the settlement of English soldiers it became known as 'Little England.' Geographically it lies in the state of North Rhine – Westphalia. The camp itself was approximately two miles from Paderborn.

Ironically, at the end of the war, the historic military base passed first into the hands of the Americans before a long-term hand-over to the British.

Normandy Barracks, Sennelager, was to be my home for approximately twenty months. Despite its attractive façade some of the buildings beyond were grim.

Following the check-in procedures at the Guardroom, I was taken together with my equally anxious colleagues to a large three-story building marked,

'RASC Training Wing & 138 Supply Company'. To all intents and purposes the two units were responsible for identical duties and were distinguished only by the different markings worn on the epaulette.

The building functioned as administration offices on the ground floor with the military staff accommodated in the rooms above. Although not the Hilton, the standard was much improved on Willems. It still meant walking about a hundred yards from my room in order to have a pee.

It was now early evening and it had been a long time since I had been fed, my stomach reminded me. I joined the informal gathering en route to the Cookhouse. Again I was pleasantly surprised by the higher standard. The food, as expected, was still very basic: meat, veg and mashed potato, but nevertheless edible and filling.

There was still time to relax on my bed afterwards. I lay, both hands resting behind my head, as my mind recalled the events of the day. It had been the longest day in my life. Was I dreaming, or could I hear the sound of a radio somewhere further down the corridor?

The Army does not grant you a lot of thinking time. Your every moment is mapped out for you. Instructions are either being bawled at you by a senior rank, or a notice board, positioned strategically would serve a similar purpose.

It was back to reality the following morning. The day began at six o'clock. No shouting or banging, I was allowed to rely on my alarm clock. A quick wash and shave, dress and off to the Cookhouse. As we, in small groups, hastened to dine, big jock Reynolds was heard to utter something to the effect that there would be no Haggis on the breakfast menu.
    ' Puts lead in your pencil,' explained Jock. Taffy Jones was quick to point out,
    'There will be nothing to write on, stuck in this hellhole.'

After breakfast it was all haste to be on the parade ground for the morning inspection. At 0900 hours I was dismissed to the offices to await further instructions.
    This was the commencement of a three-week period of intensive training. Time was to be spent on the firing range just in case some silly sod started a war! The weather at that time was freezing cold, evidenced by a couple of brass monkeys that sat on the sidelines. Other than yet more 'square bashing', we

spent our time in the classroom perfecting our typing skills and learning administration procedures as applied in BAOR.

It was about this time that the government decreed that the title British Army of the Rhine should cease in favour of British Forces Post Office. Apparently we were not to upset the nationals. Odd really, I thought, as it was these buggers that bombed my chippie.

The advanced training followed a similar pattern to that of Willems Barracks. There was, at least Monday to Friday, a routine of early- morning parades prior to classroom work designed to enhance trade skills. Much to my personal dislike, there were frequent sessions of weapon training.

An exception was made with regard to Wednesday afternoons, which was earmarked for sporting pursuits. A serious-looking young man wearing spectacles wondered if chess counted as a sport.

'No, you Pratt,' was the response.

The sports facilities were very good, with an extensive range of equipment and venues. My own preference was tennis and cricket which I had enjoyed playing at a reasonable standard before entering national service. Although it was still early spring, the weather was warm and pleasant.

My prowess at tennis was to lead to an interesting episode a little later on in my service.

***

Typically, I was ambitious as to where I would spend the rest of my time in Germany. I fancied the 'big city' life. If not Paris, why not Berlin or Hamburg, I thought? Unfortunately, suitability for a particular location was not determined by performance on the training course.

I mulled over the options for a few days until, 'Eureka.' How about making an application for a 'compassionate' posting. A posting on the grounds of bereavement. This was a facility granted to those who could prove that their personal experiences would justify special treatment. As mentioned earlier, my father had died in 1953. With hindsight, I deeply regret that I was to use my loss as an attempt to gain preference in deciding my subsequent area of service. Needless to say, it did not work.

I had met and befriended two German boys on a short holiday I had taken in the Lake District in the summer before I was called up. They had the wonderful names of Dirk Rider and Rolf Karenburg. They both lived close to

Hamburg and I envisaged being able to sample civilian life, albeit German style.

***

The scene in Sennelager was reminiscent of Aldershot, when in excess of two hundred soldiers assembled in the Physical Training Centre. Clearly this was the only venue large enough to cater for the numbers.

On this occasion it was Captain Norris who was the officer in charge of the proceedings. In his soft Irish accent he addressed the men sitting in anticipation of yet a further upheaval. Most of the postings were to towns and cities I had never even heard of.

Looking upward, as if seeking divine guidance, his gaze returned to his notes as he read, S/23092158 private Gibbs. Leaving the script to one side he continued,' I have considered your request for a posting on the grounds of compassion and regret that there is no vacancy in or near your preferred location of Hamburg.' His eyes twinkled and with a wry smile.'I have done the next best thing. You will be going to 91 Supply Depot in Berlin.'

I resisted punching the air with delight as I contemplated a prolonged stay in the former German capital, with all its secular pleasures. 91 Supply Depot of the Royal Army Service Corps was situated in the old Olympic Stadium that was home to the 1936 Olympic games. I was to be joined by two of my course colleagues, Mark Dyer and Pat Kirwen.

CHAPTER SEVEN

ONWARDS

The next day was depressing as close friends were cast asunder to serve out their remaining service many miles apart. With kitbags packed and in full uniform, the newly trained clerks and drivers were loaded on to trucks and transported to the railway station at Paderborn. The process would continue all day until the last of the men glanced back at the now familiar Guardroom for perhaps the final time.

The personnel bound for Berlin adopted a different routine. At that time, it was necessary to travel through the Russian zone of Berlin in order to gain access to the Supply Depot. This involved the train being halted as Russian guards entered the train to inspect travel documents.

The consequence was that the three of us were to spend a further few days in Sennelager awaiting instructions. It was obviously a regular occurrence as Mark, Pat and myself were quickly despatched to the offices of the Training Wing, where we were to assist the clerical staff as required.

It proved in fact to be very leisurely with a lot of spare time for other pursuits. It was to be my downfall! Most of my leisure hours in the preceding three weeks found me on the tennis court playing non-competitively with whoever was available. I had also been a spectator and watched a men's doubles match that surprisingly included Captain Norris. A fellow spectator had explained that the tall, hard-hitting member of the side was an officer in the Veterinary Corps.

CHAPTER EIGHT

NORMANDY BARRACKS

I was three days into my transitional duties when the chief clerk, Warrant Officer Emery, called me to his desk while pointing to the telephone.

'Call for you,' he snapped in an accent that I failed to recognise. I picked up the handset and heard a familiar voice say,

'Captain Norris here, report to my office immediately.'

I thought, what the hell have I done wrong now.

I saw the nameplate emblazoned on a door just a few yards from the office where I was working. 'Captain Norris DSO' and knocked. I was invited, or rather ordered, to enter. I marched in and saluted as I reached the large metal desk he was sat behind.I think I detected a faint smile as he paused and then said,

'Private Gibbs, you are not going to Berlin as planned. Bloody hell, I'm off to Hamburg after all, I thought.

'Right sir,' I said in a confident tone. 'Where am I going, sir?'

'You are to remain here on the permanent staff of the Training Wing.'

I would not have felt worse had he have placed a black hat on his head and uttered the words, 'until you are dead'. I was shell shocked, more at the thought of a prolonged stay in Sennelager than a posting to Berlin.

Captain Norris then gave his reasons, although not required to.

'Captain Wilshaw of the Veterinary Corps is leaving the army at the end of the month.' His tennis partner, of course!

'You are to take his place in the team representing Normandy Barracks. I have noticed that you play a decent game and under my guidance you will no doubt improve.'

So this is how the sodding army functions! Military strategy goes by the board in favour of tennis. Unbelievable I thought.

The officer went on to explain that tennis practice took place every Tuesday and Thursday evening at 1730 hours. Competitive matches were arranged ad hoc, including weekends, to accommodate the opposition.

'You will be excused duties when required to play,' he stated. 'And by the way you are to become assistant to Cpl. Steer as a unit Pay Clerk.'

After the initial shock and disappointment at not going to Berlin, the idea of spending many hours playing my favourite sport I regarded as adequate compensation. I fancied also that the prospect of working in the Pay Office was one of the more interesting tasks. I saluted again and made my way back to the 'General' office, only to be greeted with,

'Are you for the firing squad laddie? from Warrant Officer Emery.

'No sir, I will be joining your staff.'

'Good. Your first job is a trip down to the NAAFI for two bacon sandwiches. At the double. That is military parlance for 'quickly.'

Other than a change of room/billet, there was little difference. I was welcomed by a few of the other lads who all appeared very friendly. They all shared the common goal of demob.

The following morning I bid farewell to Mark and Steve as they set off for Berlin.

Breakfast and early morning parade over, I reported to the Pay Unit and introduced myself to Cpl. Cliff Steer, my new boss. Cliff was from Maidstone in Kent. He seemed to have the knack of dramatically changing his accent, from the 'plummy' to cockney, depending who he was talking to.

'Pay Parade' as it was referred to, took place on Thursdays at 1200 hours. This allowed three days in which to compute and prepare the Pay Roll. In addition to playing tennis, of course.

There were approximately sixty personnel that appeared on the roll, which was the combined strength of the Training Wing and 138 Supply Company.

The level of earnings to be paid varied according to rank and status. The pay of regular soldiers was always higher for the corresponding rank of a national serviceman.

Cliff proved to be a good tutor and quite soon I was able to prepare the pay myself. Just as well, as he would excuse himself with the declaration, 'I'm just pissing off for a brew.' That was termed, 'pulling rank.' I had, regardless of my rapid progress, been referred to as a 'thick sod' on a number of occasions.

In addition to paying out the wages, the Pay Office was responsible for issuing the concessionary 'cigarette cards.' During the Fifties, smoking was a popular habit for soldiers of all ages. The normal cost of cigarettes was prohibitive, relative to the pay of, particularly, national service men and therefore the cards were regarded as a valuable asset.

The effect was, that on production of a cigarette card, the vendor would sell the goods at less than half the normal retail price. They were issued in denominations of eighty and sixty. The entitlement was one hundred and forty cigarettes per week. There was then no medical evidence to put the 'frighteners' up you. I quickly realised that for the less scrupulous, this presented a rare commercial opportunity.

***

Cliff was promoted to sergeant shortly after; by no means unknown, but a fairly rare status for a national serviceman. I now saw even less of him as he frequently announced,

'I'm pissing off to the Sergeant's Mess.' He now had the facilities of the Mess at his disposal.

The Cookhouse opened for two hours in the early evening and catered for an alarming number of hungry young men who all jostled for position in the long queues that formed while waiting to be served. The customary duty sergeant ,who would take up position at the entrance in an attempt to keep some semblance of order. The Training Wing staff, other than for small groups, made little contact after normal hours.

At the end of the working day there were the normal chores to be dealt with. Uniforms had to be pressed, boots cleaned and the room cleaned and tidied. This still left plenty of time for leisure which was spent in diverse fashion including: sport, the camp cinema, the pub and indoor recreation laid on by organisations such as the NAAFI and the Church Army.

For those who chose some peace and quiet there was always your bed to lie on. This was a popular pastime made all the more pleasurable by the possession of a radio. Initially I had to rely on the goodwill of a mate to extend an invitation to share such enjoyment. There were a number of music fans. Cliff, before his transfer to the higher echelons of the sergeant's quarters, John Sawyer, Brian Wilson and Taffy Roberts being the mainstay. They were all modern jazz enthusiasts and I soon became a huge fan. *Take the A Train* by Duke Ellington, was a big favourite and used as the theme music for a late night jazz programme. There were no facilities to play records and therefore the wireless was the only form of entertainment.

The twin broadcasting stations, called the American and British Forces Network, were the most popular. There was the Sunday evergreen, Family Favourites, that attracted a huge audience. The playing of requests was combined with a link-up facility, allowing personal messages to be relayed.

The quality of sound was not great. I suppose this was because of the antiquated equipment in use. I think some had descended directly from that of William Baird had been handed down as the men returned to the UK.

My own room was like a morgue without the accompaniment of a radio and something that I was determined to remedy in the near future.

***

My first trip into the town of Paderborn occurred during an Easter bank holiday weekend. It was Saturday lunchtime and a small crowd from my own unit waited restlessly for the tram that stopped outside the main gate. Clearly half of the population of Normandy Barracks had chosen to spend their Saturday likewise.

Four of us from the Training Wing were all making our maiden voyage to town. We were pleased to be dressed in civilian clothes enabling us, we thought, to blend imperceptibly into the local population. On the contrary, our youth, short hairstyles and general demeanour were a 'give away' to the trained eye of the oppressed.

We alighted from the transport and surged towards the town centre. On joining the high street, Taffy almost immediately asked, in a loud accent,

'Have you seen what is on at the flicks?' *Rock around the Clock.'*

Cinemas in Germany are much like our own and readily recognisable. I had read in the English press that the film starring Bill Halley was enormously popular back home. It was reported that audiences were dancing in the aisles.

It was a unanimous decision to dip into our limited funds and buy a cinema ticket. Coincidentally the picture was due to start soon; we therefore joined the queue.

The Germans were more orderly or perhaps less enthusiastic than the Brits. Fighting had apparently broken out at certain venues up and down the UK. The film was great and we sang along to the group, much to the annoyance of the German members of the audience.

It was late afternoon when we, together with the other shoppers, returned to the fray. It was noticeable that the locals were loaded down with great bundles of chocolate Easter eggs.

We window gazed as we dreamed of at least owning a radio The German men's fashions also caused a longing until we examined the prices. The clothes were obviously not destined for the national serviceman's market.

There was a particular portable radio that was very popular in the Barracks. It was manufactured by Phillips and small enough to sit easily on a bedside locker. The quality of sound was superb. I was determined to accumulate sufficient funds to buy one without too much delay.

It was decided to round off the day with a gargantuan but low-cost meal. However, a more pressing need was to heed the call of nature, but where? That was the problem. None of us either spoke or could read German. I had picked up a few words in the company of my friends, Dirk and Rolf. That was to prove disastrous.

As we headed back to the main square, we caught sight of a public convenience, hardly distinguishable from our own, except of course the signs situated above the two entrance doors were in German, Heren and Damen. Clever sod me reasoned that obviously the word containing men, that is 'Damen' must be the 'Gents.' With few people in the vicinity of the loos we rushed in, eager to relieve our overloaded bladder.

'No troughs,' exclaimed one. Odd, I thought, but it was now too late to stop the process. We exited the building in quick succession only to virtually collide with an elderly lady entering the 'Damen' Four very embarrassed lads made a hasty retreat absolutely in silence.

As we tucked into our schnitzel and chips we had to share a joke and vowed to attend German language classes as soon as possible. I had lost my status as 'spokesman' but apart from that was relatively unscathed

The remainder of the Easter break flew by and was largely uneventful. I played some tennis as I was determined to justify my selection for The Barracks team.

Shortly after resuming military duties, I was made aware of a Training Exercise that was to take place for the duration of one week, commencing on the first of May.

Army Training Schemes attempted to replicate actual battle conditions. The entire unit was involved except that is for me.

Two quite different sets of circumstances came to my rescue. Schemes were no joy ride and not akin to a Scouts Outing. The ranges at Sennelager were notorious throughout West Germany. Being on them was like being on Dartmoor on an 'off day.' Even in May they could be hostile and desolate. Apart from having to sleep in a 'Palliasse' and eating all food from a mess can was not funny. A mountain of beans and corned beef was seen being loaded by the Catering Corps lads.

I suffered or, more accurately, purported to suffer, from varicose veins in my leg. I did indeed have evidence of a problem. This was sufficient excuse to avoid the long standing required in a military operation. In any event, as the Unit Pay Clerk on duty, I was automatically excused exercises in order that the important task of preparing the Pay Roll was done. An extra benefit was a 'lie-in' as there were no early- morning parades.

The Training Wing, together with the Supply Company, moved out as planned. It never ceased to amaze me how the time scale was adhered to. Chaos would reign for the few days immediately prior and then, like magic, it all fell into place.

The downside to being left behind was soon apparent. During the absence of the unit personnel, my role was titled 'holding party.' Throughout the working day, as the only clerk, I had the responsibility of handling all the communication signals between the Headquarters of the Rhine army in Monchengladbach and the Training Wing. I dreaded the thought that some silly sod would start a war that week. It took me all my time to organise a shave. Getting tanks operational was out of the question. Seven days later, my bedraggled comrades trooped back to depot. There were the usual tales to tell, most of which were either fiction or very exaggerated.

***

I still missed home terribly but learned to adapt and actually enjoy the experience.

Military duties such as 'Guard Duty and *Piqueting* occurred rarely. Although after a few short weeks of working in the wing I was instructed to perform the duty of *Piquet.* As Normandy Barracks was home to a whole variety of military and trade training it was the centre used for enhanced training of the Women's Royal Army Corps. WRACS, for short.

Naturally they had to be accommodated and the building chosen for their sleeping quarters was just two blocks away from my unit. The Army Council in their wisdom had decided that these vulnerable ladies would require protection against the lusting behaviour of the young troops in camp, anxious to share their bedrooms. For that reason, iron bars were fitted on to the bedroom windows to thwart the efforts of any randy soldier who fancied his chances.

The main door of the building was also padlocked from 1900 hours each evening. *Piquet* duty comprised four men, who in turn would patrol the block, a baseball bat in hand. They were there to guard the ladies for the reasons explained. Duty hours were from 1900 hours until 0630 hours the following morning. There was a system of duty involving two on and four hours off.

The two men on duty would then parade the block some forty yards apart. It was my first experience of   *Piqueting* and I wondered if it was really necessary.

It was approximately midnight as I strolled, occasionally stopping as I peered into the darkness in anticipation of an attack

It was freezing cold and I hopped from one foot to the other and rubbed my hands in a vain attempt to keep warm. Sod this for a game of soldiers I thought. My thoughts were interrupted by a knocking sound that appeared to be coming from one of the rooms. I glanced up at the barred window behind me and shone my torch. The sight astounded me! A so- called, vulnerable young lady appeared at the window, smiling and using her forefinger in a curling manner, which I understood was an invitation to supper.

My gaze focussed on her naked breasts, which were exposed, presumably to confirm her interest in me. Realising that she had now gained my attention, the hand signal changed and was indicating entrance by the main front door. I was staggered as I wrestled to discover an appropriate response. Bugger me! I thought those bars were designed to prevent access, now I understood they were for the safety of the 'virgin soldier.'

Without even daring to reciprocate the smile, I replaced my torch, took a firm grip of the bat and moved swiftly on. I decided, that in the best interests of military discipline, not to relate my experience to the other lads in the unit until the next day.

Needless to say, one said he would have risked seven days in the 'Glasshouse' or even the firing squad, for the same opportunity.

Volunteers for *piquet* duty shot up over the ensuing few weeks. Taffy Roberts suggested a black flag should be flown when the ladies were not in residence.

***

It was while having a cup of char, army parlance for tea, during a morning break, which was usually spent in the Church Army canteen, that I overheard a conversation. A young soldier, sitting at the same table, was speaking in a very familiar accent. A Potteries dialect is quite unique and beyond the acting skills, it seems, of most thespians.

'Are you from Stoke-on-Trent?' I interrupted.

The soldier smiled and with his twinkling blue eyes looked in my direction. It transpired that his name was Bill and by an amazing coincidence had married a girl who at one time was in my class at school. His companion was virtually abandoned in favour of firing questions at me. We became pals almost instantly. He explained that he had been posted to Germany three months ago as a driver in the Royal Army Service Corps. Despite qualifying as a driver, he worked on the camp Petrol Station, responsible to Sergeant Davies.

We hurriedly slurped the remains of our, now cold, tea and arranged to stay in touch.

We met on a regular basis thereafter, much of the time devoted to nostalgic reminiscing about home.

Bill did not share my enthusiasm for sport, which meant that weeks might elapse before a rendezvous was possible.

John Gibbs

CHAPTER   NINE

PRIVATE ENTERPRISE

Bill would occasionally visit me in my room in the Training Wing accommodation block. We talked endlessly and particularly on the subject of music. We were both fans of Ella Fitzgerald, Sarah Vaughn and other jazz greats.

'If only we had our own radio?' I said. This was a defining moment in what was to become a joint business venture/scam, in the buying and selling of radios.

Bill remarked, 'You must have access to spare cigarette concession cards, John?'

'Of course,' I replied, 'after all, I control the supply within the Unit.'

'Those little cards could become a passport to our wealth,' my friend retorted, revealing a more sinister side to his nature.

'Certainly we should be able to fund a couple of new wireless sets.'

'Bloody hell,' I exclaimed, 'let's devise a strategy.'

As a matter of procedure, I would indent for a small surplus of cards at the weekly Pay Parade. It was designed to cover the contingency of new personnel joining the unit at short notice. In addition, there were always some 'non-smokers' who did not avail themselves of the concession. It became clear that there was an opportunity to trade the cards. I would buy from the non-smoker and sell on at a profit. I wondered if Richard Branson had started this way!

From the outset, trade was brisk as the smokers eagerly snapped up the bargain deals.

There was nothing illegal in our activity, although I accept that the Army would not approve of such enterprise.

For that reason I insisted on a fairly low-key approach while sufficient to realise our modest ambition.

Bill was ideally placed as a petrol pump attendant to deliver the sales pitch while filling up the vehicles.

We purchased a small stock of second/tenth-hand radios, mostly from lads returning home at the end of their service. We tested them, of course, and if they were discovered to make a sound vaguely like music, they were effectively on sale. Some quite honestly were 'a bag of bones' but amazingly they could be sold. 'Sold as Seen' was the motto. There was certainly no six months guarantee or even six hours provided.

One of the most audacious sales we made took place during a quiet Saturday. A punter, that is potential buyer, was offered a demonstration of a particular radio. It was manufactured by Pye Limited and was massive in size. The wretched thing required a very long aerial just to obtain reception. The aerial cable was then fitted into a metal tube for enhanced performance.

The unsuspecting buyer was from a different unit, which meant that hopefully we would not subsequently meet.

Bill had explained to the potential customer,

' Reception is not too good.'

'As long as the thing produces some melodious sound, everything will be OK!'

Although not readily apparent, the demonstration required two operatives: one on the roof of the building directly above my room. The idea was to drop the aerial to the room below and feed the cable into the room via an open window.

The poor sod arrived on time and was escorted into my room. I stood anxiously by as I turned on the switch. After a few hesitant crackles, eh presto, the apparatus burst into life!

'Not great,' said the lad.

'The acoustics are rather poor in here,' I replied.

Ah well, I'll take it.' With that, I passed the huge set into his open arms. Another few bob in the kitty was my callous thought as he struggled to exit the main door. A short while later the gleaming blue eyes of Bill appeared at my door.

'He's a big bloke,' I remarked. 'Any complaints go to you.'

The extra money generated from my ill-gotten gains made service life easier to bear. I was soon able to afford larger helpings of food in the NAAFI catering facilities. This was usually after spending an evening at the camp cinema. Little regard then for the calories been consumed. Other treats included being able to participate in the organised trips at the weekend.

On one such event I journeyed to see the Eder and Mohne Dams, the scene of the daring air raids depicted in the film, The Dam Busters, starring Richard

Todd. It was fascinating to see at close quarters the aftermath of the devastation caused in that epic attack by the Royal Air Force. The repaired stonework was clearly visible and appeared like a huge postage stamp spreading across the retaining wall.

Eventually I accumulated sufficient cash to fund the purchase of a brand new radio. At the first opportunity, I made the trip into town and, with a broad grin on my face, returned with the goods. This was the single biggest buy I had ever made and outstripped the purchase of a bicycle I obtained when just fifteen years of age (made possible from the proceeds of wages earned as a newspaper delivery boy).

I was immensely proud on both occasions as I realised that my parents could not afford to provide such luxuries.

The novelty of the radio never really wore off and my ear was frequently glued to the set at all times of the day and night.

I suddenly acquired a whole new circle of friends who would find an excuse to visit my room. In order to recapture my space, I tried yawning but finally had to resort to the expression, 'piss off'. That seemed to work, other than for the 'rhino'-skinned, Roger.

CHAPTER TEN

HIGHLIGHTS

August the eighth that year is etched in my memory, perhaps because of my silly sense of humour. That morning, several of the lads were enjoying a tea break in the main office when Sergeant Worboys breezed in. He stood to attention and faced his small audience of expectant clerks. Worboys was a regular soldier, with a wry sense of humour.

'Here it comes,' remarked Corporal Owen, also a regular.

Worboys began:'It was the eighth of the eighth, at round about eight. I was N.C.O., I.C., main gate.

Private Jones came in late.'

'Jones, you're late.'

'What time is it?'

'Tattoo.'

He then said,'Ta ta,' and pissed off.

'That's the last I've seen of the bastard, Sir!'

Everyone howled with laughter and even all this time later, I still smile at the thought.

***

October 1955, the Army bestowed on me, my only military honour. Lost in a sea of mundane notices, there appeared on the General Office board the following announcement. S/23092158 Private Gibbs will, wef (with effect from) Monday the 2nd November 1955 is promoted to the rank of Corporal. I was to report the following day to the office of Captain Norris.

The procedure was little more than verbal notification and an exchange of salutes. Following the short ceremony, my first action was to collect my spare tunic from the room and present it to the German lady seamstress for the job of stitching on the stripes. I accepted the sardonic comments from the lads in exchange for a promise of free drinks the following weekend.

Being a mercenary sod, my first reaction to the promotion was to calculate the effect on my weekly pay. I hasten to add that I was not an ardent drinker but had certainly by now succumbed to the evils of the flesh. Mother would not approve as alcohol was rarely ever seen in the household.

'Only for medicinal purposes,' was the expression mother used.

The pub frequented by mainly servicemen was situated directly opposite the camp main gate. The snag was that it was in the glare of the Military Policemen who would regularly visit the Guardroom. It was not unknown to see them in the pub. 'Just to keep an eye on things' was the excuse made. I naively thought they were in for the odd game of dominoes.

***

I was still in the habit of attending church on Sunday mornings. It was an ecumenical church. Only the Catholics and Jews had their own place of worship. The services were conducted by the camp padre, with whom I became friendly. I remember my first act of worship was to plead forgiveness for the previous evening's drinking.

The practice of avoiding normal duties by false or 'make-believe' claims, were referred to as 'skiving.'

For me an opportunity arose from my connection with the camp church. The padre informed me that a religious instruction course was to be held and would I wish to attend.

The venue was a delightful country house located in glorious countryside approximately thirty miles from Sennelager. Not wishing to miss out, I applied immediately.

I obtained the necessary permission to attend for the duration of four days. The setting proved to be idyllic, and the ambience, on a par with the finest English Guest Houses.

Coincidentally, the padre from Normandy Barracks was to take his turn in conducting the course. He invited me to travel with him in his army VW Beetle. It was no Roller but a vast improvement on a two-ton truck, the usual mode of road transport .En route, I discovered his passion for cricket and therefore was able to avoid any reference to theology.

On arrival at the centre I was directed to the reception area for registration as the padre trotted off in a different direction.

I looked up from my writing and for a moment thought I had died and gone to heaven. On the opposite side of the counter a stunning- looking lady had taken up a position. She was tall, slim and her dark hair cascaded down to her shoulders.

Not normally short of words, I mumbled a response to her questions.

I wondered if this was the devil's way of distracting the students from the moral philosophy that was to follow.

Dinner that evening was served with wine in a magnificent dining room. I could imagine that many a battle could have been planned here. Outside were beautiful gardens that surrounded a small swimming pool.

The weather was sunny and warm, which enhanced the scenery.

The four days passed all too quickly and it was with a tinge of sadness that I threw my luggage into the waiting vehicle. I had escaped reality for a while and now it was back to playing soldiers again.

CHAPTER ELEVEN

WHAT THE SOLDIER SAW NEXT

My friendship with Bill continued and produced another memorable episode in fall from grace, Bill spotted me in the NAAFI one morning and immediately grabbed my attention.

'I have been asked to 'baby-sit' on Saturday night by my boss, Sergeant Davies.'

'What's the score?' I asked, using army speak.

'The Serge and his wife have a nice little pad in the married quarters on camp. They want me to keep an eye on the kids while they get pissed in the Sergeants Mess. They may even manage a game of Tombola.

'I suppose we all have our standards,' I said a bit pompously. 'A touch of civilian life would make a welcome break.'

Bill added jam to the sandwich by promising to stock up on copious amounts of food and booze.

Now absolutely convinced, I confirmed a time and address with him before resuming my mid-morning snack.

The following Saturday evening I arrived at Sergeant Davies' quarters and rang the bell. There was no response and I glanced at the crumpled paper in my hand as I checked the number on the door. Bill eventually appeared, the smile on his face, which I am sure was a permanent fixture aimed in my direction.

'Sorry for the delay,' he remarked, 'couldn't find a bottle opener.'

A crisis had obviously been averted as the appropriate piece of kit was now in his hand.

The apartment was deserted apart from the two small boys who, I was informed, were sleeping soundly.

'Let battle commence,' said Bill as, with an adroit flick of on hand, he simultaneously turned on the radio and reached for a bottle of lager. In addition to the radio we had the use of a 'radiogram.' No telly of course. I examined the pile of vinyl records and arranged them in order of my listening

preference. I came across a long- playing record of The Glen Miller Story,'
which was all the rage at the time.

'Cheers,' said Bill as we settled down for an eventful night.

Left to our own devices, we embarked on an evening of small talk, music
and the dreaded liquid refreshment. Come midnight we were both feeling the
effects, which resulted in a crude attempt at crooning and some sharp
exchanges on the topic of football. Bill was a supporter of the other league team
in our home city, namely, Port Vale FC.

I had drifted into a sleep when the loud noise of the front door being
opened brought me to life abruptly. Bill had obviously heard Mr Davies and
his wife Doreen fumbling with the door keys and had decided to greet them.
The small sitting room was at the other end of the property, where we were
spending our time. I could not distinguish conversation but the sound of
raised, boozy voices together with the odd spate of raucous laughter was
sufficient to determine that a good night had been had by all. Approximately
twenty minutes had elapsed when there was a door banging sound as Mr
Davies, I gathered, left the party.

At this time Bill had made no attempt to invite me to join the revelry and I
decided that I was definitely *persona non-gratis* in the proceedings. After what
must have been another thirty minutes I heard the sound of a duet. I crept into
the dimly lit corridor, which led to the lounge area. A light shone through the
partly open door. I paused and listened to the words of the ballad, *Ramona* in
what was a vain attempt to sing by the giggly couple.

I decided to investigate further as curiosity welled up inside me. I tiptoed
along the hallway and reached the open door. Silence had now replaced the
singing as the minutes ticked by. I was able to peer round the door and
immediately wished I hadn't. The scene ahead left me gob-smacked. A naked
Bill was spread-eagled on top of a hapless Mrs Davies. Fortunately I was not
seen, or so I thought.

I did a hasty retreat to the sitting room and poured a generous measure of
the Sergeant's whisky. Head in hands, I sought to rationalise what I had
witnessed, I thought of poor Patricia, my old school friend. I decided not to
moralise with my mate and business partner and simply play along with the
experience.

Bill eventually returned to join me when I wondered if his first words
would be by way of an apology for his unusual behaviour. He was now fully

dressed of course and other than blurriness of the eyes he appeared remarkably fit. Typically nonchalant, he asked,' Are are you ready, sorry for the delay?'

Here was a man who was ostensibly happily married and who had almost certainly just committed adultery with his bosses' wife, acting as though he had been delayed shopping. I never did receive a full explanation as to the events that took place at the end of a corridor. Neither, for some strange reason, was I invited to baby-sit again.

CHAPTER TWELVE

CHRISTMAS LEAVE

My attention was aroused as I scanned the notice board in the clerk's general office. It was early December and already there were thoughts of Christmas. The idea of spending the festive season away from home had filled me with horror.

The notice read: Arrangements have been made to transport qualifying personnel wishing to travel to the UK for the Christmas holiday Flights will depart Dusseldorf airport on the 23rd December to London, Heathrow, and returning at 1600 hours on the 30th December. Those interested parties must submit an application to the Chief Clerk, Warrant Officer Emery, by the 15th December.

I was due for home leave anyway so I ought to qualify, I reasoned. The cost was twelve pounds for the flights plus the rail fares I would incur.

Thanks to the cigarette card venture, I was able to afford it. I might even have enough money to include a number of Christmas presents.

'Have you ever flown before?' questioned Warrant Officer Emery as I handed in my completed application.

'Bikes tend not to fly, sir,' I uttered, more in humour than arrogance.

'You will be in a Dakota, not the most luxurious aircraft but I don't suppose you will notice.'

'Too right sir,' I said. ' I've never seen a Dakota!'

A few days later a notice appeared, indicating that my application for Christmas leave had been authorised.

It was my first experience of flying and I quietly had the 'chits' at the prospect.

My fears were compounded when on the day of departure the whole of West Germany, it seemed, was covered in a blanket of fog. The flight from Dusseldorf amazingly got away on time.

This pretence at an aircraft thundered along the icy runway as I stared out of the window at the gloom beyond. Visibility was virtually nil. That added to my fear as I felt the plane lifting off the ground. The pilot must have 'cats eyes' I thought.

The contents of my stomach were in conflict with my throat as the air turbulence wreaked havoc. The lad occupying the seat next to me was built forward with his head resting on the back of his outstretched hands. I swore I heard the words, 'Our Father.'

Fortunately England was experiencing marginally better weather and although very cold was free of fog. The Dakota had landed like an overgrown grasshopper that jumped along the tarmac before coming to rest outside a Terminal building. The onward trip home was by coach and seemed to take for ever. There were no motorways then and, despite the early hours, the city was busy with traffic and progress was very slow. I was cheered by the thought that it was Christmas and I was to be home. With that thought I drifted off to sleep.

I must have slept for over two hours as I spotted the sign for Birmingham, 'fifteen miles.' Still having a long way to travel to my home in north Staffordshire I attempted to pass the time by reading. It was, after all, Christmas Eve and I contemplated the days ahead.

I would fulfil my obligations to my folks and spend some time chatting to them. I would then make my way to the home of my girlfriend, Doreen, who lived a few miles away in Hanley. My welcome there as always was overwhelming with hugs and kisses from all the females and handshakes with the men. Doreen had five sisters, all of whom had made the effort to be part of the reception party.

It was an incredible feeling to be back with the people that meant so much to me. Christmas came and went in a blur of television and turkey and it was soon time to be planning the return trip. On the morning I was due to leave I felt very depressed at the thought of going. I suddenly announced an outrageous plan to give me more time.

My tooth had been playing up and although not life threatening, I decided I would call the dentist

I talked my way into an appointment and within an hour I was sitting in the dentist's chair. Mr Wain, my dental surgeon, prodded and poked around so as to locate the offending molar.

'I need to fill a tooth, young man,' said a smiling Mr Wain.

He looked as though he had just found gold. 'I will inject the gum with cocaine in order to freeze it.'

It was early afternoon before I was to resume consumption of sausage rolls and mince pies. Ah well, not too heavy a price to pay for an extended break. I had obtained a note from the dentist which confirmed my treatment and which I would present on my return.

I was able to arrange a flight to Dusseldorf on the second of January that meant I had the bonus of being with the family for the New Year celebrations. The extra days passed very quickly and with misty eyes I was on my way back. I dreaded my reception at the other end. The duty sergeant was unlikely to be as friendly as my potential mother-in-law. I looked again at the note, unfit to travel. I bet the cynical swine's don't believe me I thought.

I arrived back in camp in the early hours of the morning, with only the 'duty clerk' available in the main office. I left my note with him and headed for my bed, a very weary soldier.

At the end of roll call later that morning a voice boomed out,' Corporal Gibbs you are to report to Captain Tate's office following the parade.'

'Shit, what now?'

I was paraded in front of the fierce- looking officer in the usual manner and duly saluted.

The gist of it was, that he was not satisfied with my excuse for returning to my unit late.

The army relied on the all-embracing rule of The Queen's Regulations, conduct subject to the good order of military discipline.

The punishment was: 'You will be confined to barracks for a period of seven days, plus three days of extra guard duty.'

I was then marched out of the office and dismissed. I questioned his parentage as I focussed on the horrors ahead.

I was not a regular drinker and, therefore, the confinement to barracks was not a problem. My main dread was the humiliation of being made to scrub tables and paint coal. Yes, it did happen.

***

Time now seemed to drag and, despite the enjoyable interludes, I still yearned for my release. The more fortunate members of the staff, with little time left to serve, would yell, 'roll on demob' designed to cause further depression.

Another opportunity presented itself to take a break. On the notice board appeared details of educational classes to be held in an army training establishment. A range of subjects were offered that would culminate in an examination for the (O) level, G.C.E.

The distraction of a course would pass the time more quickly, plus the fact that I needed to add to my small tally of passes.

The venue was Hone, approximately fifty miles from my unit. I discovered that Hone was formerly Belsen, the notorious concentration camp.

Knowing that I was to be treading the steps of the wartime horrors was a double-edged sword. It was fascinating yet very emotional.

My application to attend was successful and I was soon in receipt of travel documents for the ensuing rail journey. The training school had been built virtually on the site of Belsen camp. On arrival I detected an eerie, ghostly atmosphere that I found disturbing.

The Germans had changed the name of the town for obvious reasons. From what I witnessed the locals appeared unaware of its graphic history.

I shared accommodation with three lads from the East Surrey regiment. The infantry units were often regarded as having the less intelligent but this was not the case with my temporary colleagues. They spoke with posh accents and were a little 'far back.'

It transpired that a friend of mine, Rex Sawyer from the RASC Training Wing, was a former student of the college. He was a free-lance journalist by profession and had written a feature for the *Daily Mirror*, entitled, *Belsen, Ten Years After*. He was able to include a photograph of a human scull, discovered on the site of the army school.

Rex was now nearing demob and was anxious to resume his work in the media. Thankfully my studies occupied much of my thoughts during my three-week stay. My spirits were lifted on my return by an altogether contrasting experience.

CHAPTER THIRTEEN

THE VIRGIN SOLDIER

It was early autumn and despite a chilly breeze that swept across the parade ground, it was one of those mornings when it felt good to be alive.

I was participating in the early morning routine parade and roll call that took place every weekday.

Approximately forty yards away and walking along the road which formed the perimeter of the parade ground, I spotted three uniformed ladies, obviously members of the Women's Royal Army Corps, walking en route to their eating quarters. Forty sets of eyes, bulging like chapel hat-pegs strained to get a better look. Rather like a bird of prey about to kill: the concentration was intense.

There were audible sighs of shock as my gaze focussed on one particular member of the group. At the head and strutting like a Vogue model, was a lady displaying the largest bosom imaginable. Although she was wearing uniform, including a tunic, her generous breasts wobbled, to the delight of the sex-starved young men who were spellbound at the sight.

The excitement was all over very quickly as she disappeared in the distance, however the memory lingered on, so much so that the lady now described, as 'the one with the big knockers' was the subject of conversation at the morning NAFFI break.

Much to everyone's disappointment it was not to become a regular habit and the afore mentioned lady was soon just a memory.

That was until two weeks later. It was Saturday and I had been detailed as duty clerk for the weekend. It meant I was confined for much of the time to the block of offices occupied by the Training Wing.

As duty clerk, it was mandatory that I sleep in the 'general office' over night. A crude camp bed was assembled for my benefit: it was usual to make temporary use of the desk allocated to Warrant Officer Emery, the chief clerk, that of course was while he got pissed in the Mess.

The one consolation was that I was able to plug in my radio to deflect from the boredom. I had eaten early in order to start work at my desk by 1800 hours. It was going to be a long night, I thought, as I flicked through a number of messages that were for my attention. I was to remain on duty until 0700 hours the following morning.

Saturday night was always the worst night to be working and ensconced in the building. The front door was left unlocked and there was always constant pedestrian traffic throughout the night as the drunk and battle-scarred drinkers stumbled back to their billets.

On one occasion a bleary eyed soldier, having missed the stairs, decided to seek the company of the poor sod on duty. Following his unreasonable demands for a drink, I was forced to escort him to his room. Fortunately he was too inebriated to offer any resistance.

I got back to my office in time to hear Duke Ellington playing *Take the A Train'* It was now midnight and I decided that, as war was not imminent, I would settle down for the night. I turned out the main light with only the glow of the corridor lights outside to reflect their beams. I was fully dressed and lay on top of the bed in the hope that I might doze off to sleep.

I was awakened by a loud noise as some silly bugger slammed the front door. I peered at my watch and the time read, two am. Someone was now walking along the corridor in the direction of my office. I was both curious and nervous as to which inconsiderate mortal was to invade my sleeping time. The door opened and in came large breasts, quickly followed by a familiar looking lady. I stared into the eyes of the female soldier that had caused so much interest two weeks before. For a moment I thought I had died and gone to heaven.

She was dressed on this occasion in civilian clothes and was wearing a skirt and jumper, which enhanced her feminine charms.

I was about to ask if I could help when she blurted out her apologies for interrupting me, explaining that she had to send an important message to her family in the UK. There was a telegraphic system that was controlled from the general office.

She had obviously been drinking as her conversation was slightly slurred and was punctuated by fits of giggles.

'Doris is my name,' she said as she offered me her hand.

She explained that she had spent the evening in the Sergeant's Mess and having forgotten on the way out, decided she would call on the return journey to her quarters

The sight of Doris mesmerised me as she put the seduction process in overdrive.

I was no Clarke Gable, but fuelled by alcohol the lady found me sufficiently attractive to make a play. In a voice that was barely audible, she whispered that she did not have a man in her life. With her chest looming large above me I could fully understand why. I felt like putty in her hands as she attempted to join me on the bed. If only mother could see me now, I thought! She then asked the burning question, 'Do you like my breasts?' It was rather like asking Lester Piggott if he liked horses.

I had previous experience of passionate kissing and cuddling but this was beyond belief.

The last time I felt this threatened, Eric had been approaching with a bottle of 'Indian Ink.' With no stool available, I jumped off the bed while suggesting impolitely that she leave.

My mates would have died for a similar opportunity. I was not being self-righteous. I was simply naïve, a virgin soldier.

***.

As spring turned into summer in 1956, my mood changed as I contemplated release and my return to civilian life. I was due to return to the UK in early November and even the prospect of crossing the North Sea again was no deterrent.

That summer I devoted all my spare time to playing tennis and cricket. However, I managed to find the time to increase the turnover of cigarette card sales.

With less than four months to serve, I became what the national service refers to as 'demob happy.'

CHAPTER FOURTEEN

ALMOST A REAL SOLDIER

In November of that year, an event of seismic proportions occurred. I stared at the front page of *The Daily Telegraph* and read *War in the Canal Zone*. Col. Nasser, who had in July nationalised the Suez Canal, was the focus of attention by the British government.

The selfish bastard, I thought, as this could thwart my chances of demob. The scene was of small groups of men, huddled together as they debated the prospects. Regardless of the gloom cast by events unfolding, we managed to maintain a sense of humour. An invasion by the combined forces of Britain and France were to invade the area by means of dropping troops and equipment in an operation to free the canal, a vital link between the Middle East and Europe.

Israel had invaded the Sinai in October of that year and were to rely on the British and French for support.

Meanwhile, life in the Training Wing carried on as normally as possible in the circumstances. Men had to get paid and fortunately continue to smoke and listen to the radio.

'All good for business,' I remarked to Bill.

During a period while duty clerk, I took down an important signal that came from the Headquarters of The BOAR at Monchengladbach. It was requesting volunteers, both officers and other ranks, that had parachute qualifications. Clearly they were to be at the forefront of the proposed attack. The very thought of diving into space from an aircraft gave me the heebie-jeebies. Some silly sods, however, were fearless and even enjoyed the idea.

In addition to the Parachute regiment itself, service personnel from all sections of the forces were able to attempt qualification and attain the right to display their 'Wings'. The wings, depicting a descending parachute, were worn with pride. Ironically enough the first ever descent was over Paris.

Second in command of 138 Supply Company, which was accommodated together with the Training Wing, was a Captain Tate. He was an evil and miserable sod. Captain Tate was short in stature but built like a heavyweight wrestler. His constant companion was a boxer dog, equally fearless but better looking. The officer's claim to fame was that he had been a trialist for the Welsh rugby team and he sported the wings of the parachute regiment on his sleeve.

It was my mate Taffy Roberts who came up with a devious plot to oust the said officer from our midst.

'Let's put his name forward as a volunteer for the drop.'

'Absolutely brilliant,' I replied.

I had access to all the personal records, including the all-important regimental number. Within a matter of days, an unknowing Captain Tate forwarded an application as a volunteer in response to the request. Taffy claimed that the bugger had dropped us in the shit many times and it was now, his turn. Despite his protestations, he was soon on his way.

No tears were shed that morning as we witnessed his departure during the early morning parade. He got into the passenger seat of his army style, VW Beetle and was quickly joined by his one admirer, the boxer. His driver saluted before taking up position behind the wheel. With smoke streaming from the exhaust, he was off.

'That's enough,' yelled the drill corporal in response to the whistles that were heard. My stomach churned as I realised that I may be caught up in all this. Not as a volunteer, I hasten to add.

Throughout and following the skirmish a great deal of front-page news appeared and questions were asked in The House of Commons. Fortunately for me the United Nations imposed a ceasefire in November. It had been a close call and I breathed a sigh of relief.

My fears were again raised when the Russians attempted to defer my demobilisation by invading Hungary, supposedly to quell a revolt.

It was difficult to understand that two years had elapsed and National Service was soon to become a memory, etched on my mind.

Later that month I, along with a number of others received our instructions for release.

As I prepared to leave on that chilly autumn morning, my happiness was tinged with sadness. I was never again to enjoy the companionship, banter and laughter that were at the heart of my service experience.

I jumped up on to the back of the waiting army truck as Lance Corporal Reynolds threw in my kit bag. I think he had a tear in his eye as we shook hands and slapped each other on the back. Ninian Reynolds was a Scot that hailed from Bute on the island of Rothsay. A giant of a man, not usually given to emotion, he had joined me as assistant in the Pay Office when Cliff Steer was demobbed. He now had assumed overall charge. I had tutored him well, particularly in the art of cigarette card distribution.

I did not look back. I was experiencing the same feelings I had experienced in November 1954.

CHAPTER FIFTEEN

THE JOURNEY HOME

Immediately I embarked on the long train journey to the Hook of Holland, The realisation of impending freedom set in. The time spent in Sennelager soon became a fond memory. Not for the geography, but the people I encountered, some good, some bad, but memorable nonetheless.

I peered out of the window as the huge train, like a metal dinosaur, trundled out of the station. 'Auf Weidersein,' I whispered to myself. It was undoubtedly the adrenalin that kept me awake throughout the trip.

The sea crossing, made during daylight hours, was marginally better than my first crossing. I marvelled at the sight of the cliffs of Dover as they appeared on the horizon. They stood majestically, their white chalk making them easily visible. Robert Browning's words sprung to mind, 'Oh to be in England.'

The final leg of the journey home was to be broken by the call of curiosity. We pulled into Victoria station to chaotic scenes. Wives and girlfriends hugged and kissed their partners. Like an enormous plague of locusts, the mainly khaki clad servicemen hastened along the platform in pursuit of waiting transport.

Taffy Roberts was my one surviving comrade from the unit and it was he that reminded me of the call regarded as 'a must' for those leaving the army and passing via Victoria.
'We must have a pint in 'The Dirty Duck' or 'Hole in the Wall' as it was sometimes called.'
This notorious London pub had apparently played host to hundreds of outgoing servicemen. The place was heaving as we raised our glasses with a toast to 'civvy street.'
We said our last farewells and were soon on our way home. For me, Stoke-on-Trent was the destination. I couldn't believe it.

CHAPTER SIXTEEN

LOOKING BACK

I am a Gemini by birth sign and the traits attributed to Gemini truly reflect my personality. I had decided against returning to my former employer, but instead joined the staff of British Thompson Houston Limited as a junior draughtsman.

I was in any event entitled to demob leave of one week at full pay. There was no cigarette card allowance, unfortunately.

I did visit my old work colleagues at Birketts and was surprised to find there were no changes in personnel. With much backslapping and banter the memories came flooding back. Alan shouted, 'Did you get to Paris?'

'No' I replied.'

'Where then?'

'Sennelager,' I said.

'Damn me, sod that for a game of soldiers.' he said, or words to that effect.

National service had been an important part of my life. There were times when I hated it and the degrading stupidity. The way in which young men were treated was cruel and unnecessary. However, I entered as a boy and emerged as a man and a little wiser.

The Suez crises blew over as quickly as it arose and perhaps with the exception of Prime Minister, Anthony Eden, it was largely forgotten.

The services provide a structure to your life. Without the option to wander, one's routine is orderly and conforms to a pattern. On termination of my service I had to rely on self-discipline and think for myself.

After a few weeks I decided to visit my barber, Mr Tatton. It was the usual Saturday morning that I strolled into his shop and was quickly invited to take a seat. Little appeared to have changed as he said,' Short *back and sides* young man?'

'No, thanks, I'm out.'

Short Back and Sides

With the cape in place to protect my new clothes, I watched in the mirror and smiled back with glee.

Part of UKUnpublished.co.uk .CO.UK

UKBookland gives you the opportunity to purchase all of the books published by UKUnpublished.

Do you want to find out a bit more about your favourite UKUnpublished Author?

Find other books they have written?

PLUS – UKBookland offers all the books at Excellent Discounts to the Recommended Retail Price!

You can find UKBookland at www.ukbookland.co.uk

Find out more about **John Gibbs** and his books.

Are you an Author?

Do you want to see your book in print?

Please look at the UKUnpublished website:
www.ukunpublished.co.uk

Let the World Share Your Imagination

Lightning Source UK Ltd.
Milton Keynes UK
172782UK00001B/27/P